I0478529

CHRISTMAS ON A BUDGET

HOW TO GET CHRISTMAS DECORATIONS, GIFTS AND MORE FOR LESS

WRITTEN BY: MARIE COLLINS

Be sure to check out the free Easy Holiday Cookies blog to help make this Christmas the best one yet:

EasyHolidayCookies.com

TABLE OF CONTENTS

PREPARING FOR THE HOLIDAYS THE RIGHT WAY

Christmas can be one of the most joyous times of the year, but it can also be one of the most stressful. During the holiday season, it's easy to overspend without realizing it, and find yourself financially strained.

If this is you, or could be you, I have some good news!

It's actually easier than you think to have a fabulous festive holiday without spending a pretty penny. If spending less and saving more is one of your goals this season and for the year ahead, than is book is for you. You'll learn the right way to prepare for the holidays and how to have a very MERRY 'Christmas on a Budget.'

Although the word 'budget' can make some individuals cringe it's just a matter of mindset. To budget simply means you're working with a limit. Everyone is working with a limit whether they're conscious of it or not. Doing Christmas on a budget is all about being smart with your money and generously giving without depleting your bank account.

WHY HAVING A HOLIDAY BUDGET IS IMPORTANT ...

Gifts, decorations, food and all those little expenses that occur during the holiday season, can quickly add up if you're not careful.

We all know that modern day marketing is built around pulling on people's heart strings and playing with their emotions. During Christmas we see a lot of this, especially with TV, radio and print advertising.

During this time of the year we're bombarded with slogans and lines in Ads like:

"Show mom you love her by buying her _____ ... this Christmas."

"Give your children their best Christmas yet by buying them _____ ..."

"The one you love deserves to be spoilt this year. Buy her a _____ ..."

"Forget the socks and jocks, what he really wants from Santa is a _____ ..."

"Don't let YOUR children miss out! You must buy them a _____ ... this year."

Have you ever noticed that the gifts that they suggest you buy, often cost hundreds of dollars and sometimes even thousands of dollars? It is natural to feel guilty if you are contemplating spending say $10 or $30 or on that person, when you see advertising telling you that if you truly love someone you will spend hundreds of dollars on them. The marketing guru's have weaved their magic, and before you know it you've passed your planned spending limit and are buying an more expensive present just so you don't feel guilty!

The holidays can also be an emotional time for many of us. It's easy to start reflecting on your relationships and situation and become emotional, which can trigger you to overspend when shopping.

If you have a close family member that is no longer around, during this time of the year can be rough. It's common to feel depressed and try to overcompensate for the loss through retail therapy.

However, you have to remind yourself that overspending is only a temporary fix that you'll regret later. Avoiding the pitfalls of the holidays and incorporating a budget will not only save you tons of money but it will free you from the stress and burden of compounding debt that often follows shoppers well into the New Year.

It's important to remember the reason for the season. Avoid getting caught up in the consumerism of Christmas.

The holidays are about love, family, giving and being thankful for all that you have. It's not about name brands, merchandise and who got who what.

Don't let your emotions get the best of you. Ignore all of the propaganda, advertising, and hype that makes Christmas a commercial enterprise. Focus on the true meaning of Christmas instead and make this time of the year full of traditions, joy, happiness, caring, and sharing. Stay strong, plan ahead and take action to ensure this holiday is the greatest one yet. You got this!

Doing Christmas on a budget will help alleviate unnecessary stress and make sure the holiday isn't as much of a financial strain. You'll save money on buying gifts, decorations and avoid the Christmas rush, when many retail stores often raise their prices.

Having a set spending limit for food, gifts and other necessities, and keeping to it can significantly help sharpen your budgeting techni☐ue in the future too.

Buying small gifts and using creativity to make your own gifts can often be fun and also cost effective. As a bonus, friends and family will appreciate the thought that has gone into the homemade gift!

Now warm up some hot cocoa. Pull out some paper and a pencil and let's get started:

The first step to having a successful Christmas on a budget is planning ahead. Similar to any other style of budget planning, you have to sit down and make a list. I like to make mine a bit festive with a few candy cane doodles but you can create your list however you want.

If you prefer to use a computer and type it up in Word or Text File that's fine too. You can even make your list on a notepad app on your Smartphone, the way you compose it is entirely up to you. I recommend taking a minute to look into your bank balances and finances and see how much you're working with.

Were you preparing for the holidays and have a little money set back? If not, how much do you have? How much do you need to continue paying bills as usual without any hiccups along the way into the New Year? How much can you afford to spend this Christmas?

Make sure your calculation includes not only gifts but holiday décor and additional food and entertainment during the break.

Once you have a good estimate, write that number at the top of the paper. I like to circle it for dramatics … but you can underline or bold it if you'd prefer. You want this number to not just be visible but to stand out while you're creating your budget.

On the left side of the paper start listing the names of all the people you need to buy gifts for. Don't write what they want or what you're going to get them. Just their name.

Now at the very top of the paper make a mini category list with the following: males, females, kids and for those animal lovers you can add the category pets.

Go down your list and tally the number for each and list it. So next to males it should be the number of males on your list you need to get gifts for and etc.

This brief category will help make shopping easier so you don't get side-tracked. If you know you need to buy X amount of gifts for the men in your life like father, husband, brother and brother in-law you can save valuable money and time by making X amount of gifts for that gender. Or by buying a particular gift item in bulk or in different varieties depending on their preferences and age.

In general it's also a good trick to use to keep you from running around the store from one aisle to the next searching for a gift for your mother and then into a different department for your brother and then back over the women's department for a gift for your sister in-law.

Knowing your numbers in quantity, genders and money can make the ordeal of shopping a breeze.

After you've tallied your numbers. Look at your list and all of the people you need to get presents for. For each person, next to their name write down one interest, theme and or item they like.

For example my niece loves the color pink, she's very feminine like anything girly and like most teens is very into jewelry.

So next to her name would be: pink, girly, jewelry. You can list all three or just one or two depending on how much of an idea you already have on what to get them. Don't list any specific item, keep it general.

Go back down your list and start listing the max amount of money you're willing and able to spend on each person on your list.

Don't let the numbers make you feel guilty. We're being economical and practical. Just because you're setting a max limit for your dad at $20 doesn't mean he hasn't been an awesome dad. Remember, you're not Santa Claus.

This isn't about who's been naughty or nice. It's about a budget and working with what you have. Most parents could care less what you get them.

Often it's our own emotional baggage and insecurities that make us think we have to prove our love and appreciation by getting the perfect gift. It's not true.

So, don't worry. Even if your max limit for someone is $5, in this book you'll learn how to turn that small amount into some really great gifts.

Don't Jingle All The Way

About now, you're looking over your list and thinking, "what about my kids? I mean I have this max limit for them and I know for a fact that it won't allow me to buy them the official 'so-in-so' they been begging for."

Don't be pressured into feeling that you are a bad parent if you don't buy your children the latest gadget or toy that has been advertised to death over the weeks leading up to Christmas.

Like the classic Arnold Schwarzenegger movie, 'Jingle All The Way,' where he's racing through town trying to get his son the hottest toy of the year, the Turbo-Man doll.

In the end, all the boy really cared about was spending time with his dad.

Kids are simple, they want to be entertained and loved. You can do both of those easily on a budget. If you've planned ahead and have enough saved for that one item your kid really wants than great!

However if you don't have it, do not go into debt over it. That toy that they really want ... they're going to play with it for a couple days and it'll be tossed in the back of a closet somewhere while you're struggling to pay the electric bill for the month of January.

Don't do it. They will be okay if they don't get it. Children are resilient. It won't be the end of the world, especially if you teach them early on that the holidays is not about getting gifts, it's about giving and love.

Doing Christmas on a budget means buying your children what you can afford. Remember time spent with a child is worth a million gifts.

Only buy your children a couple gifts - especially if you have lots of family and friends who will also be buying presents for them. If you don't you can use the tips in our gift buying section to get your kids the most for your buck.

For now though, let's concentrate on completing our list. Ask your children to choose two or three gifts that they want, advising them (only if they are older children) that if the gift is too expensive they may not get it.

Add those requests to your list. Although you may not be able to get that exact gift, knowing will give you a good idea of the type of gifts to search for.

Help your children to write a present list themselves of who they want to give gifts to. Try to teach your children to budget their allowances to ensure they have the money to buy what they want to give. Encourage them to make gifts and cards for friends, family, classmates and teachers instead of spending money.

CREATE A NEW LOW-COST FAMILY TRADITION

During this time of the year the kids are out of school and it's easy to go over your budget paying for little outings to keep them busy. Remember your total at the top of your list. That number includes entertainment expenses.

Below are some great ideas and activities that you can do with your family and children during the holiday season to not only bond but that will create some awesome memories and save money in the process:

- Take a walk / drive to see the Christmas lights in your neighbourhood
- Have a sing a long and sing Christmas carols
- Play board games or do jig saw puzzles together
- Go to a Carols by candlelight
- Read Christmas stories as a family
- Watch Christmas DVD's (if you don't already own some of these, it's a great investment. Walmart usually have Christmas cartoons and films discounted as low as $2 in their DVD bins)
- Participate in free activities put on around your neighborhood - church pageant, Christmas carols, lighting of the Christmas tree, Christmas parades, etc
- Give some time to help out a local charity
- Help sell Christmas cards / products for your local charity
- Send a card to someone in a nursing home / shelter / lonely neighbour
- Visit an elderly lonely neighbour
- Making Christmas presents for friends and family

- Making Christmas cards
- Making Christmas treats - mince pies, shortbread, cookies, cakes, chocolates
- Hanging an advent calendar
- Going to a service at your local church / place of worship
- Hanging some Christmas lights
- Decorating the house and tree with home made decorations / ornaments

Following these helpful tips will make this Christmas an enjoyable one. Preparing for the holidays the right way will allow you to spend your New Year relaxing and achieving your savings goals, instead of struggling to pay off unnecessary debt.

INEXPENSIVE CHRISTMAS DECORATING 101

We've created our Christmas on a Budget shopping list, now it's time to set that aside and begin your holiday décor inventory list. You may be wondering, why do I need to do that?

Well, most likely you have no idea what you have stored away. Most people don't. We tend to re-buy things when we don't really need to due to the fact that we've forgotten we already have it or simply have no clue where we last placed it.

Taking stock of what you already have packed away in boxes or storage marked X-MAS can save you a lot of money and time. Plus, once you have a holiday décor inventory list made you can use it every year to help manage your Christmas decorating budget.

When it comes down to inexpensive Christmas decorating, taking inventory of what you already have is the first step.

Creating Your Holiday Décor Inventory List

Again, grab a pencil or pen and some paper or whatever you prefer to create your holiday décor inventory list. Go down to your basement, garage, closet or storage unit and pull out all of your Christmas decorations.

Sort through it all and list everything that you have. Anything that is in good condition place a checkmark by it. Anything that is in poor condition or that you think has probably has seen its last Christmas, circle or highlight it.

During this process if you think of any item that you believe you need and do not have write it down.

Examine the items circled and the new ones you added to the list. These are the décor items that you'll most likely need to buy inexpensive versions of, re-purpose to make like new or create yourself.

Since most decorations are fun to buy during the holidays, such as Christmas LED lights, ornaments, garlands, wrappings, Christmas trees, rope lights, Christmas balls, and many more, thus, you need to be careful and consider your budget when choosing to buy these things.

On your inventory list prioritize by importance the decorations that you really need. Does it really need to be replaced or can some little TLC bring it back to life?

Most items can be reused and turned into a new kind of holiday décor with a little bit of creativity and a few inexpensive materials.

Once you've finished taking inventory, you can start shopping and creating.

WHERE TO BUY INEXPENSIVE HOLIDAY DECORATIONS

You'd be surprise how many people go to major department and signature retail stores like the Christmas Tree Shop for their holiday decorations. Although these shops have a wide variety of beautiful Christmas decorations, they are also overpriced.

You're paying for the brand name, the festive ambiance and convenience of shopping at the mall or in an all-Christmas shop. All of which are unnecessary. A wreath is a wreath. An ornament is an ornament and a candy cane is a ... candy cane regardless of where you purchased it from.

You can buy or make decorations that are just as attractive and festive as the items available in the mall. Finding good quality decorations for Christmas at reasonable prices is not difficult. You just have to be patient and know where to look.

Dollar Store has a great selection of Christmas decor and ornaments, but it's hidden among the clutter. If you're willing to take the time to look you can get a lot of fantastic festive decorations for a fraction of the cost. Garlands, candles, ribbons, flowers, sprigs, ornaments, table accents, mugs, dishes, and even a few great gifts can all be bought for just $1.

Below are a few helpful tips to remember when buying decorations:

1. Buying beautiful ribbons (which can be purchased at the dollar store, Walmart, or any craft store) is a great way to fill out your tree without spending a fortune on expensive ornaments. Simply pick 1-2 ribbon colors that match your color theme and wrap or drape them around your tree. This will not only spruce up the tree by adding color, but it will also give it a fuller appearance, so you don't need as many ornaments to decorate.
2. Instead of buying extra little gifts and trinkets to fill up Christmas Stockings, stuff the bottoms with plastic grocery bags.

3. If you don't have a lot of Xmas decoration. You can shop at the thrift stores after Xmas and during the summer yard sales to find great deals for under $5.

Walmart is another great place to find inexpensive holiday décor. Walmart is notorious for their clearance sales, rollback prices and special buys. You can find a lot of good deals for reduced priced holiday decorations at Walmart online and in-store.

Before I venture out into the stores I like to do an online search first to get a good idea of what they have.

To see some of the special deals available, in the Walmart search box, enter terms like 'Christmas Decorations Clearance' or 'Holiday Décor Clearance' and change the sort filter to 'Low to High.'

You'll find all types of ornaments, wall décor, wreaths, and other festive decorations on sale. Often you can find large assortments of ornaments for relatively low prices at Walmart.

Walgreens and Rite Aid or any local drugstore will have Christmas decorations for sale also. It's usually just one or two aisles in the drugstore dedicated to whichever holiday season it happens to be. If you stop and browse through these holiday aisles you'll notice that many of the products are very high quality and reasonably priced.

Rarely does any particular item, in the drugstore cost a lot. Taking advantage of these hidden gems will make it easy to find inexpensive holiday décor to fit your budget.

Your local craft store is another hot spot to find great deals on Christmas decorations. The secret to not overspending in a craft store and getting the most for your money is to go prepared.

Never walk into a craft store without a list and solid game plan for what you're going to create. It's easy to get side-tracked by all the cool crafts and ready-to-go products on display.

Similar to a department store display, everything in the craft store will beckon you to buy and hang it. But going blindly into a crafter's paradise can quickly lead to trouble.

Avoid going over your set spending limit. Thoroughly research your holiday décor project and the current sales before you attempt to shop.

Wreath foams are a great example of this. In the local craft store they can cost up to $12 but you can make your own by buying pool noodles and taping it together with some duct tape to form a circle.

Remember the craft store has multiple skill level products. Depending on what you're looking for, you usually find several different options.

From inexpensive supplies to pre-formed supplies to finished products. Having a list and idea of what you need prior can help you save money and get exactly what you need.

GETTING CRAFTY WITH THE DÉCOR

You don't have to be Martha Stewart to create your festive holiday decor. Anyone can do it with the right inexpensive supplies and know how. I want to share with you some of my favorite ways to decorate for the holidays to help you hang that perfect wreath, make your front door a grand holiday entry and spruce up your living room to reflect your inner holiday cheer.

Using Pine Cones

Pine cones are natural, inexpensive and charming items to use in your Christmas decorating projects. They work great for country Christmas decorating ideas or if you just want to add a more rustic style to your holiday décor.

There are several easy ways to work pinecones into your holiday decorating themes. You can make a pine cone wreath. To do so only use several different sized pine cones, thread them into a circle tightly together and bind them to a grapevine wreath or any wreath of your choice. Tie a pretty red ribbon, attach red berries and you have a country style Christmas wreath.

Another great idea is to dip pinecones in red or green paint, sprinkle silver glitter on them and let them dry. Tie red ribbons and sprigs of evergreen to the cones and hang them on your windows, doorknobs or even drape them over the back of dining chairs for a festive look.

Stepping off the Beaten Path

Traditional Christmas trees are always beautiful, but there is nothing wrong with stepping off the beaten path and choosing a Christmas tree theme that fits your personality or are adorned in your favorite things.

Some very creative Christmas trees that are sure to draw attention are trees with decorations focused on beaches, birds such as doves or owls, burlap and rustic décor, candy themes and nutcracker theme trees just to name a few. Simply use your imagination.

Think of a style that truly fits you and then just start adding the ornaments you need that centralize around your theme. If you have children that love Hello Kitty or Sponge Bob either of these style ornaments would be great Christmas decorating themes for your holiday tree.

Choosing Colors & Fillers

Another way to save money when decorating is to keep it simple. Choose 1-3 colors as your holiday décor theme. For example, my color theme this year is Blue, Sliver and White.

So instead of buying additional boxes of blue and silver ornaments to help decorate my tree, I purchase ribbon. Both ribbons and artificial sprigs can be used as fillers when you're decorating your tree to reduce the need for ornaments.

The local craft store, Dollar Tree, and Walmart often have rolls of ribbon for sale throughout the year for as low as $1. I found some really beautiful rolls of blue and shiny silver ribbons for $1 each in a discount bin.

Sprigs are usually only cost a dollar and can be found at all of the stores mentioned above as well.

Wrapping decorative ribbon around your tree will give it a beautiful flowy effect but also lessen the need to have a lot of ornament balls which can be expensive if you have a large tree that you're decorating.

Sticking sprigs into your tree will help fill up the gaps and make your tree look fuller as well. It's a really inexpensive way to decorate your tree without spending a lot of money.

The front door of homes is often left neglected during the holidays, but it should not be so. The entry way to your home is the place your guests will get the first impression of you, your home and your overall personality. You do not want your guests to feel uninvited during the holidays. Add some festivity to your home and create your own festive door.

There are several ways to create an inviting front door for the holidays that is sure to leave a lasting impression. You can add more life to your door by draping garland over the door frame and allow it to swag down each side.

Add bows, Christmas bells or Christmas balls to your garland to finish the classy look. Use holiday style foil or paper and encase your front door. Shinny designs such as red, silver, gold or green add an elegant touch.

Accessorize the look by adding poinsettia on each side of your door, large nut crackers, Santa sleighs, toy bags, baskets of gifts or other Christmas themed décor to complete the look. Try to use decorations that you already own, purchased inexpensively or made.

DIY Christmas Wreaths & More

Your home just doesn't say, 'Welcome ... Happy Holidays' without a beautiful wreath hanging on the door. Right?! However, if you're doing Christmas on a budget, spending the extra $20 to $60 on a door decoration is not an option. Especially, since you can easily make your own wreaths at a fraction of the cost with a little know-how and creativity.

Money Saving Tip Alert: Make your own Christmas Wreaths with inexpensive supplies at Dollar Tree or your local craft store.

Making your own holiday wreaths is easier than you think. Most of the supplies that you need to make a DIY Christmas wreath is available at Dollar Tree. You can literally make your own custom wreath for less than ten dollars by using holiday decorations from the Dollar Tree.

In this section, I'll show you how to make two beautiful but very different holiday themed wreaths while working on a budget. The first is the Traditional garland holiday wreath and the second is a unique ribbon style wreath that can class up any entry.

TRADITIONAL GARLAND HOLIDAY WREATH W/ FLOWERS

Supplies:

- Wreath Wire Frame (You can find these at Dollar Tree or local craft store like Hobby Lobby or even Walmart)
- 15 feet Garland Packages (1-2 packages for smaller wreaths / 3-4 packages for larger wreaths)
- Plastic Flowers (2 bouquets, but you can use single one stem flowers if you prefer as well)

- Plastic Decorations (1-2)
- Tinsel Stems

Tools Required: Scissors or Wire Cutters

To get started, simply take a trip to your local Dollar Tree and beeline to their holiday decoration section. They usually have wreath wire frames available in small to larger sizes.

Pick the size you want but remember for larger wreaths you will need more garland. Garland is one of the coolest items they have at the Dollar Tree during this time of the season. Search for the rope garland hanging in packs marked 15 feet.

Guestimate how many you need to cover your wreath wire. If it's a really small wreath wire, you'll just need one. If it's small to medium, you'll need 2 maybe 3 packages at the most and if it's large like the one I made in the photo you'll need 3-4 packages of 15 feet of garland.

Everything is a dollar so if you're unsure and like me, hate having to make multiple trips to the store, then grab an extra pack to be sure.

You can use it later to decorate your stairs or fireplace mantel if you didn't really need it. On their wall, they have a large collection of plastic flowers.

Decide before hand what color theme you want to use for your wreath and select the flowers and decorations that stand out the most to you.

They have a lot of great little decorations from glittery pinecones and various bouquets of flowers to birds and berries. The bouquets are the stems with multiple flowers attached.

To stay within budget, try to buy the flower bouquets instead of the single individual flowers.

We will be cutting the flowers off of the stems, so you'll have more flowers to work with if you grab the bouquet type. Select the decorations and a pack of tinsel stems if you don't already have them.

Okay, time to get your DIY on! Take out your packages of garland and start unwinding them. Once you have one long 15 feet of garland at your disposal, begin wrapping it around your wreath wire.

Tightly secure the last inch of the garland around the frame with a neat tuck and grab your next package of garland. Repeat the process until you have the entire wreath wrapped in garland. Now it's time for the fun part, decorating. Pull out your plastic flowers and decorations.

Take out a pair of sturdy scissors or wire cutters and snip the flowers off of the stem leaving about 1 to 2 inches of stem at the end. If you're using two bouquets with 4 flowers connected to one stem, you should end up with a total of 8 flowers to use.

Do the same with any decoration if necessary. Now, decorate the wreath by sticking the flowers and decorations directly into the wrapped garland. Once you have a stunning wreath worthy of display in any of the top department stores.

Make a loop on the back for hanging by weaving a tinsel stem into the top back of the wreath and tying it into a loop. For a larger loop, use two tinsel stems. Weave one into the back of the wreath and take the other and knot it into a circle and securely tie together. The end result will be a beautiful traditional garland wreath.

I absolutely love this wreath because you can use throughout the year. Since the flowers and decorations are not glued in, you can take them out and switch add in different ones to reflect any particular season or color theme.

EASY RIBBON & BOW HOLIDAY WREATH

Supplies:

Foam Circle Wreath Frame (Available at most places that sell crafts and the Dollar Tree when in stock)

- Holiday Ribbon (2 rolls, colors of your choice)

Tools Required: Hot Glue Gun, Scissors

This DIY Christmas wreath is not only one of the easiest but it also has the least amount of supplies.

The Easy Ribbon & Bow Holiday Wreath is an easy DIY project that can be done quickly with minimal supplies, assuming you already have hot glue gun at home.

If you don't you can buy a mini one priced at around $7 at your local craft store or Walmart.

Once you have your tools together, you'll need to buy a foam circle wreath frame and 2 rolls of ribbon.

Foam circle wreaths sell out quickly at the Dollar Tree during the holiday season. If they're out, then visit your local craft store for one.

Ribbons are sold almost everywhere and at Dollar Tree and many crafts stores you can find bins of them in various colors for sale for $1 or even less. It's a great deal.

For this simple but elegant wreath, you'll need two rolls of ribbons. Each should be a different color or vary in shade. Select one roll of ribbon to use as the base color and the other as the accent.

Warm up your hot glue gun and squeeze a small amount of glue onto the back of the foam circle where you'd like to start wrapping.

Then carefully, press the tail end of the ribbon on top securing it. Begin to wrap the ribbon around the foam frame until it's completely covered. Squeeze another small amount of glue to seal the end of the ribbon and trim if necessary.

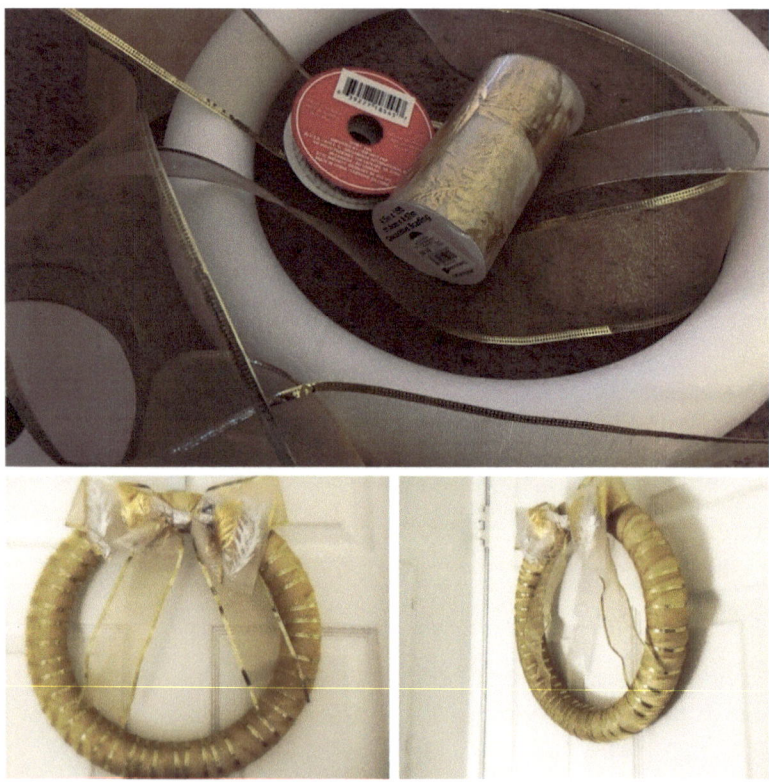

Now take the extra ribbon leftover and your accent ribbon and make a bow. You can watch this great YouTube video, right here on how to make a bow. Once you have your bow, squeeze another drop of glue where you want your bow and press to secure it.

To make a hook for hanging. Cut 3-4 inches of your accent ribbon and fold into thirds or half lengthwise depending on its width.

Then tie a knot at each end and glue the knots to the back of the wreath to form a loop. Make sure you press hard and let the glue dry before attempting to hang.

Another great wreath idea and alternate supply is the Pool Noodle Wreath. Instead of using a foam wreath form from a craft store that can sometimes be pricey depending on the size you choose, you can use pool noodles.

Pool noodles can be purchased very cheaply at hardware stores, Amazon, Target, Walmart and many other retailers.

You only need one to create a foam wreath form and some duct tape. Simply form the noodle into a circle and attach the ends together by wrapping with duct tape.

Now you have your own foam wreath form. You can make a beautiful elegant ribbon style wreath like the one above or you can make an ornament wreath using old Christmas ornaments that you no longer need.

Grab your hot glue gun and begin to glue the ornaments around the wreath form until it's completely covered. Begin with the outermost edges and work your way up and around to the inner circle.

You'll need a lot of ornaments but the final product is absolutely stunning. You can even wrap around lights for an added touch.

DECORATIVE MIRROR PLATE / CANDLE HOLDER

Another great décor that you can create for only a few dollars is a decorative mirror plate. All you need is a hot glue gun, a clear glass plate (Dollar Tree), a small round mirror (available at Dollar Tree), two bags of colored gemstones of your choice (also available at the Dollar Tree, Walmart, or any craft store).

Before you begin, you'll need to do a little bit of prep. First peel off any price tag stickers on your plate and mirror. Clean your glass mirror and set aside. Take out your handy dandy glue gun and bag of gemstones.

Glue your glass mirror to the middle of the plate. Press firmly to secure. Then begin squeezing one drop of glue and placing a gemstone.

Continue to go around the mirror gluing the same colored gemstone.

For the next row, use a different color and continue gluing around the mirror. Alternate colors for every row until the entire plate is covered with beautiful gemstones.

Now you have a stunning decorative plate for the holidays or any time of the year.

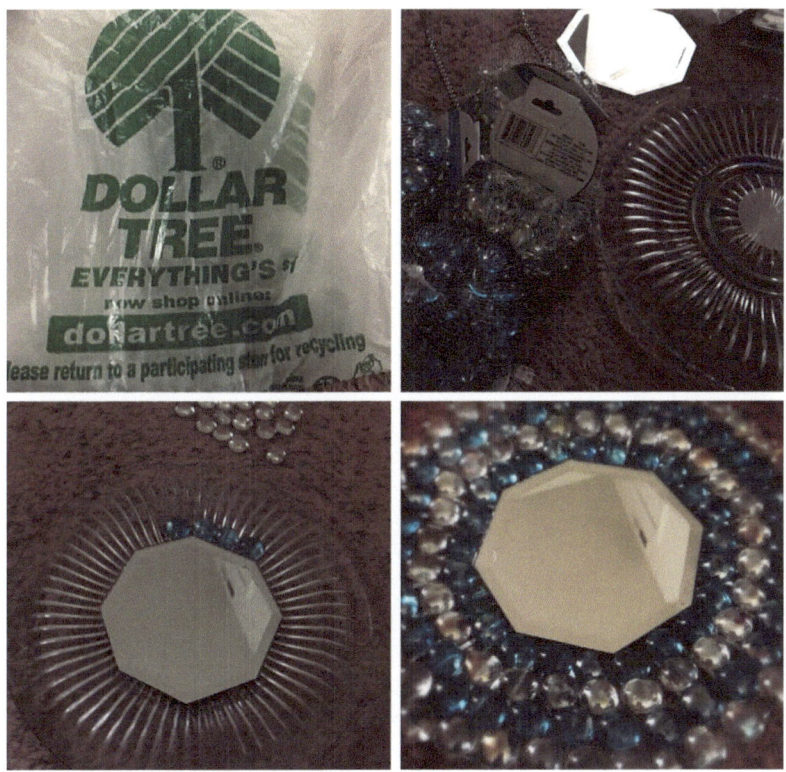

You can use a stand and place it on a table a dresser as decorative piece or you can lay it flat on an end table. Place a matching candle in the middle or add a bowl of holiday candy. This DIY item can also be given away as a gift!

Another way to really add to your Christmas decor is to swap out old photos in frames you already own with holiday themed printable.

All you have to do is go onto Google Images and type in holiday printable and a ton of free downloads will pop up. Copy, paste, resize and simply print out.

Just a few pops of Christmas printable will really make your home look festive.

You can also print out pintables for your fireplace mantle to hang as a streamer or banner with holiday inspired words like 'Let it Snow' on it.

There's a lot you can do for free if you're crafty about it.

GIFT GIVING ON A BUDGET

Gifting at Christmas time turns into a chore if you have no plan, wait until the last second, and run out of Christmas spirit (or never had any to begin with).

After all, gift giving celebrates the birth of Christ and reminds us that we are giving to the people in our lives we love and appreciate. When you forget the celebratory nature of Christmas, shopping for Christmas gifts also becomes tedious and frustrating, especially if you're working with a budget.

There are several stores that are ideal when you're celebrating Christmas on a budget such as Walmart, Target, 5 Below, Dollar Store, Walgreens, and Rite Aid. We'll touch base on each of these retail stores and what you can get there for relatively cheap.

Socks, blankets, booties/ slippers, candy, hot cocoa, tea, jars, coffee mugs, plates, and gift sets, make great inexpensive gifts for both genders. You can save a lot of money by putting together your own gift baskets or gift sets.

The Dollar Store and Walmart have a great selection of inexpensive jars and coffee mugs that you can buy for $1 or so. Simply fill it with some holiday candy like peppermints, add some packets of hot cocoa and maybe a pair of fuzzy booties or socks wrapped with a ribbon standing up in a nice display and you have an instant gift.

One box of hot cocoa and package of candy can make two or three little instant gifts, depending on the size of mugs or jars used. You can use the travel items like miniature lotion, makeup, nail polish, lip gloss to create mini festive gift baskets in jars or mugs too.

Places like Walmart, target, Walgreens, and Rite Aid are excellent for finding gift sets. They also have inexpensive kitchen items. Rite Aid has a really great selection of personal grills, toasters, bacon fryers etc.

Walmart's infamous DVD bins are also great places to find quick economical gifts to give. Plus, who doesn't like a good movie.

Create a festive cosmetic gift set to give. Simply buy fake snow (available at the Dollar Store or Craft shop for $1) or you can even use cotton ball to line the bottom of the clear jar.

Then add a couple bottles of nail polishes or lipsticks or whatever cosmetics you wish, preferably travel size. Wrap a holiday themed ribbon around it and you'll have a very cute present for less.

You can do the same with a coffee mug but instead of cosmetics stuff with tea, candy, and cookies. Cozy treat-filled slippers and Christmas cookie cans are two great examples of how you can use items you have around the house and a few new things to make a great instant gift.

Cozy Treat-Filled Slippers

For this inexpensive gift idea all you need is a pair of cozy slippers, festive ribbon, and several travel size items or treats.

Simply stuff the slipper halfway with tissue paper and then place a bottle of nail polish, eos lip balm, and snack size package of Rocher chocolates or any type of candy you prefer.

Then neatly tie the slippers together into a bow using your matching holiday ribbon.

Christmas Cookie Cans

Christmas cookie cans are another great inexpensive gift idea that you can make using old empty Pringles cans. Lightly wash them out and let them air dry.

Then get your some festive scrap book paper or gift wrapping paper and cover the Pringles can. You can use tape or glue to secure it to the can.

Take some beautiful ribbon that you think goes well with the paper design and wrap it into a bow around the can. You can secure it with a little drop of glue if necessary.

Personalize with a hanging name tag or small ornament. Stuff the can with either home baked cookies or an inexpensive package of cookies from the Dollar Store or local drugstore.

This is a great gift to give at parties or to co-workers. Everyone will be impressed by the stunning packaging and your craftiness.

If you have someone on your shopping list that's a book lover, you can buy great used discounted books at thriftbooks.com, goodwill or your local thrift store.

Take the dust jacket off if it has a worn appearance and gift wrap. They make great gifts for any book enthusiasts on your list. Be sure to pick out a book on a topic that they enjoy.

How to Find Gift Ideas

When it comes to finding great gift ideas, the internet can be a life-saver. Google a category of gifts to get ideas; online stores typically have types of categories called "Gifts for... " lists.

For example, the first person on your list is a female friend who works in an office as a paralegal, dresses impeccably, and is a fitness fanatic. Online, you can find lists of gifts for women, gifts for those interested in fitness, and gifts for the office.

Pinterest is a great social media platform to use to find gift ideas. Everything is centered on shopping and crafts so it's easy to find awesome ideas.

Check out the explore gift ideas section or search specifically for 'inexpensive gift ideas' or 'DIY gift ideas' and you'll find thousands.

CHRISTMAS SHOPPING TIPS

Now that you have a pretty good idea of what you need, what you can buy and what you can create let's dive deeper into the world of Christmas shopping.

First off, you have to make it a priority to get your holiday shopping done as early as possible. Like the saying goes, "the early bird, catches the worm."

You want to be that early bird, in order to beat the crowds and get the best deals. Little rare known fact, they always hike up the prices for last minute shoppers, so even though the tag says 'sale' it's not the same deal that was listed before.

So make it a priority to be finished with Xmas shopping a week before the holiday if not way sooner. It'll save you headaches, stress, and give you bragging rights!

Don't follow the drones and high tale it to the mall to do your holiday shopping. There are no real deals at the mall. All of the items are already overpriced.

They simply knock them down to a slightly decent price. It's an illusion that you're getting a steal. When you're doing Christmas on a budget stay clear of department stores and shop at discount places.

Walmart, Five Below, Target are all great places to start. Don't be afraid to stop at your local thrift shop or Dollar store either. They often have amazing deals if you take the time to really look.

If you can fit it into your budget, gift cards are okay under certain circumstances, like the person who has everything and the children who live in another state. Be sure the gift card is for a place/store they have access to.

If you are strapped for money and close to the end of your spending limit, consider giving personalize coupons for services like babysitting, gardening, grocery shopping. Then follow through on the promise.

You can make a really festive coupon book that your friends and family members will appreciate. Simply google 'coupon templates' or 'coupon book templates' online.

You can save the file, alter and print out. Cut them out and tape or glue them onto a really striking piece of scrapbook paper that is holiday themed.

Cut them out so they look like little individual cards. Then take another sheet of scrapbook paper and fold into book. You can do this multiple ways.

A quick method to do is to fold the paper in half and then open. Then fold it into a third from the bottom, creating a pocket across the sheet. Seal the edges of the flaps on the far right and left side with a little bit of glue or tape.

Fold back in half following the crease that is already visible and you have yourself a book. Add a festive personalize holiday tag on the front and insert your coupons.

This is a great gift to give to a sister or family member with kids who you know could use a free babysitter every now and again. It's also free, so why not!?

ONLINE SHOPPING TIPS

Regardless of what the security experts say, I shop online exclusively. I hate mall crowds and rushed shopping. When you shop online, try to always search for clearance and sales items. Check them out first before you begin looking for a specific item. You never know. You might find a gift that's in the same category of what you're looking that's available for a lot less.

Amazon and Walmart two of my favorite places to shop online. They both have a massive selection of virtually anything and you can always find good deals.

Try using rebate programs like Ebates when you shop and coupon codes for other shops online. You can often save 10-20% and get huge discounts on shipping costs with certain codes.

If you're shopping online at Walmart you can save on shipping by buying the item online and picking it up at your nearest Walmart. This is also a great time-saver, allowing you to avoid the long lines at the register.

If you shop online, be certain to order in plenty of time to wrap. Also, keep track of where you bought what items.

FINDING TOYS & THE BEST DISCOUNT DEALS

If you are a parent, doting aunt or uncle, older sibling, family friend or do-gooder who simply wants to make a tiny tot happy, you may have experienced a dilemma when it comes to finding the right toys for children while on a budget.

There are plenty of children's toys lined up in store shelves and neatly stacked on display tables but many of them are as expensive as $100 to $150.

Choosing ones that are reasonable priced, age-appropriate and enjoyable can be very challenging. So, where do you begin?

Toys are meant to be fun items to play with, so scouting for them must also be a fun event. Buying playthings for kids can be truly entertaining as long as you know what to look for and where to find it.

Take time to think about what kind of toy you wish to give a youngster. A little wisdom goes a long way when it comes to giving toys to little ones. Remember it's okay if you don't get them the hottest toy of the year.

Kids just like getting stuff. So keep that in mind and avoid feeling guilty if name brand items aren't an option in your budget. You child can still have a wonderful holiday even if you're working with a budget.

Try to buy a little bit here or there or early if you can. Toys are the cheapest during the summer months. So if you can be an early bird and start buying one or two items each month during June through August and stashing it away in your closet or somewhere they can't find it.

Your kid will look like they're spoiled rotten with all of the gifts under the tree. If you weren't able to get that big of a jump start on holiday shopping try to start as early as you can.

Utilize coupons and rebate apps. Become a couponer. Yes, there are coupons for toys! We seldom take advantage of them but they do exist. Search online and in your local newspapers for deals. You never know what you'll find available at a killer discount.

Target has a really good holiday promotion that they do yearly with digital coupons. Target Cartwheel has a toy on sale 50% each day during the holiday season. Take advantage of this deal and check daily. You can also find great deals on toys online on Walmart and Amazon.

To save even more money use the rebate app Ebates whenever you shop online. You can end up getting a big fat check after the holidays. It's worth trying.

Mix and Match and shop around. It's easy to try to get everything at one place, but you can save if you mix and match your gift items, especially toys.

For example, the Dollar Store has tons of $1 Barbie dolls, but they don't come with any nice clothes or accessories like the expensive ones do at retail shops. You can buy several inexpensive toys at the dollar store and then purchase a beautiful Mattel Barbie accessory kit at Walmart or Target.

Five Below is also a great place to shop for kids toys and gifts for teens. Everything is $5 so you can really buy a lot of toys and items while staying within a tight budget.

They have scarves, craft kits, electronic gadgets and room décor that make excellent gifts for teens. And they have tons of toys like the popular Shopskins, stuff animals, dolls, coloring books, action figures, toy cars, trucks and more.

BONUS: HOLIDAY TIPS & TRICKS

Holiday tips to remember to save money and have stress free Christmas on a Budget:

Know your priorities. Plan out everything ahead of time and take a hard look at your "to do" list and be critical. Make sure you are spending time on your most valued priorities, whatever they are.

For me, that means ensuring lots of time spent with friends and family over the holidays. It also means I go full out during the month of November on my professional responsibilities to give me space during the busy holiday season.

Make a plan. "What gets focused on, get's done." Having a plan provides structure and focus and ensures you get to do all the things you want to do vs must do.

My December calendar fills up long before December rolls around mostly with activities I schedule in advance to make sure the activities I most want to engage in are on the plan. I also free my calendar from professional responsibilities after December 15th to allow me to unplug from work and focus on personal pleasures.

Get organized. Avoid last minute gift shopping. Make your gift list early and then pick things up on opportunity. I make a list for everything.

The gift list. The list of food for each of the events/dinners we host or contribute to. The "to do" list. I also like to organize whatever I can to make it easier not only this year but in future years as well.

Christmas tree ornaments that go into neatly organized boxes and stored away from year to year under the staircase. Being well-organized can save you money as well. If you know what you have and where it's at it'll prevent you from re-buying things that you do not need.

Start Early. Buy toys in the summer months June - August that's when they're the cheapest, store them away in the basement or hide in a closet until the holiday season.

Use Coupons & Rebates. When you shop online, sign up for Ebates and go through the ebates site to earn bonus cash. You'll be shocked when you get a big fat check in the mail in January.

You can sign up for Ebates through the link listed on the reference page, if you don't already have an account. It's completely free. Similar to grocery rebate apps like iBotta and Checkout51 you earn cash back for shopping and purchasing particular products.

I also recommend checking out them out too for food purchases during the holiday and all year round. It's another great way to save.

Keep it simple. Simplify wherever you can. This may mean fewer gift exchanges or cut back on the number of greeting cards you send out.

Manage your stress. Make sure you get enough sleep and you relax whenever you can. It's helpful to stick to your regular exercise routine throughout the holidays especially if you indulge in extra food or drink.

Think about organizing a fun group activity that will combine relaxation, exercise and family time all in one event like a skating party, a toboggan party, or a bowling party.

Christmas on a budget is an effective way to enjoy the holidays without depleting your bank account. You've worked hard all year and this is the time to sit back and celebrate with your loved ones, not dig yourself further into debt.

Remember to plan ahead, shop early and at discount shops, and if you can make it or reuse it, do so. Use the tips and strategies in this book to help you have a very merry 'Christmas on a Budget.'

RESOURCE & WEBSITE REFERENCES

Below are a list of websites and resources mentioned in the 'Christmas on a Budget' book:

- How to Make a Bow (YouTube Video) - https://www.youtube.com/watch?v=xejV0-8heCk
- Ebates – https://www.ebates.com/rf.do?referrerid=0dUIfG4O 3POzqggxxZB7hw%3D%3D&eeid=29772
- Amazon – https://www.amazon.com
- Walmart – https://www.walmart.com/
- iBotta – https://ibotta.com/
- Checkout51 – https://www.checkout51.com/
- Five Below – https://www.fivebelow.com/
- Dollar Tree/ Dollar Store – https://www.dollartree.com/
- Hobby Lobby – http://www.hobbylobby.com/
- Pinterest - https://www.pinterest.com
- Walgreens – https://www.walgreens.com/
- Rite Aid – https://www.riteaid.com/
- Christmas Tree Shops - http://www.christmastreeshops.com/
- Easy Holiday Cookies - http://www.easyholidaycookies.com/
- Couponing for Beginners Guide - http://amzn.to/2eTkXZ4

FOR MORE MONEY SAVING TIPS

Learn how to use coupons and find the best deals on not just your holiday shopping but grocery and everyday items throughout the year as well.

If you're unfamiliar with couponing or are new to discount shopping I recommend checking out the following book:

Couponing for Beginners Guide: How to Start Couponing and Save Money on Groceries - http://amzn.to/2eTkXZ4

ONE LAST THING...

If you enjoyed this book or found it useful I'd be very grateful if you'd post a short review on Amazon. Your support really does make a difference and I read all the reviews personally so I can get your feedback and make this book even better.

Thanks again for your support!